INTER~~~~
WI·
A
PEST

MAX THOMPSON

MORE BOOKS BY MAX THOMPSON
AVAILABLE AT AMAZON AND OTHER FINE RETAILERS

For all the really cool kitties and their People who have been cheering me on since the very beginning of *The Psychokitty Speaks Out,* all the ones who found me along the way, and the friends I've found who will be with me all the way to the next great adventure. You guys rock.

1

BEFORE WE GET TO TALKING...

A long time ago in an apartment not so far away, after having been forced to endure the M-word as many times as were the number of years I'd been alive, my world came crashing down in the form of a walking, squeaky, little black puff of fur called Buddah Pest. Now, no one consulted me about his acquisition; one day I was enjoying my solitary life with a long hallway that suited my solitary galloping needs, three really big bedrooms in which I could take naps and go on nip trips, and I could leave my food on the plate to save for later, because no one currently in residence would molest it. The next day...Buddah.

Now, I did not know on that day exactly what was waiting for me behind closed door #1. I only knew that it smelled funny, squeaked, and had tiny sharp claws that reached under the door and stole my favorite red nip toy. There were no immediate introductions, not even after I had deduced that something was up and requested the door be opened so that I could see what lurked behind. Because they wanted to be careful, the people determined there should be a waiting period of a week or more, because whatever that thing was, it came with cooties.

They were incredibly careful about washing their hands after visiting that tiny-clawed furry thing, scrubbing up to their elbows, not touching me or any of my things after handling it. Sometimes, clothing was changed. Whatever it had, they did not want to expose me, but when it was symptom-free, they determined that it was time. We would finally meet.

Into the room went a tiny cage, and I waited in the living room, filled with anticipation and curiosity. They all seemed terribly excited for me to meet the creature with the tiny sharp claws, and to be honest, I was also a bit excited. I had no idea what it could be, other than it was not likely to be edible because, while it was real, live and fresh, it was not dead, and I only consumed real live fresh dead meats.

A few minutes later, out came the cage, and quivering in its center was a black fluff that resembled the darker shade of things which accumulated under the bed. It squealed in an absurdly high pitch, and as I inched closer it occurred to me that I could sneeze out a bigger ball of fur than this little thing. I was careful, because regardless of size, this thing might be capable of immense horrors, and I believe in being wary and prepared. But what I saw before me was so small, so fragile, that any fear I felt melted away, and I got close, sniffing.

This was not so bad.

His name, I came to learn, was Buddah—and yes, the name is intentionally misspelled—and he was presented as if his residence was something · to celebrate. And in the moment, I thought it was a nifty idea. He'd been in a kill shelter, rescued by the SPCA, and then adopted as a graduation gift for the Younger Human.

This was a brand-new kitten with no preconceived notions about life and how his would go. This was possibility. I could mold him into a shiny black image of me, he would do my bidding, and over time I would teach him the ways of the world.

But then I sneezed, and everything changed.

2

If you've followed my blog and other books, you know what happened: I got sick, so very sick, so sick that there was genuine concern that I would not live to see my 4th birthday, which was just a few weeks away. And while I was busy trying to not die, Buddah was busy growing and had no one to teach him how to be a cat. Without that foundation, he went a little bit nuts, and combined with the typical kitten frenzy, I often heard a person sigh, "What are we going to do about Buddah?"

I was too sick to voice my opinion: *send him back*. I wasn't eating, barely drinking, I moved like a 90-year-old man after losing the rodeo bull riding competition, and he was full of energy and play—and had decided I was a fine toy to abuse. He attacked, he bit, he tried to ride me down the hall like a pony. He had no concept of Big Kitty vs. Little Kitty, and I had nothing left in reserve to knock him over and pin him down, like a good older kitty would. He needed structure and a leader, and I couldn't provide that for him.

He'd been taken from his mother far too soon, and truly did not know how to cat.

If I hadn't gotten sick, and stayed sick for so long, I could have taught him.

Long story short, he never learned and has always been a few sandwiches short of a full picnic. He never learned respect, not for me, not for the people, and went about life as if we were all playthings and scratching posts. He bit, clawed, screamed, jumped on me, and regularly attacked the Woman.

He once sank his teeth into her arm, from pointy tip to his gross little gums.

But they let him stay.

The Woman learned to not react when his teeth went deep into her arm; instead, she held him tight and close, like a football, and waited until he let go. He was never sorry about what he did, mostly because he had zero concept that he was hurting anyone. He reacted to stimuli negatively and did not have the spare brain cells to grasp that his responses were inappropriate, and he was lucky to not be launched out the back door. No one blamed him for that because he truly *did not know*.

He's always been excitable; he's always been—to put it nicely— a bit dim. But he's not nonstop mayhem and he has moments when he's quiet and sweet; I'd be lying if I didn't admit that the People love him as much as they love me. He loves them; I can see that. But he's also Satan wrapped in fur, and the contrasts are exhausting.

Today, May 2019, he's 14 years old, and I'm about to turn 18. We're both old men, and we realize that at this point, either one of us could run off to the Bridge first. I've had my say over the years, in my blog *The PsychoKitty Speaks Out*, and in several books, but it's time for Buddah to put his mark on the world, and perhaps leave it a little better than it was when he got here.

He tried just writing a book of his own, his memoirs, but froze at the keyboard because he frankly cannot sit still long enough to pluck thoughts from his brain and type them onto virtual paper. So I promised I would ask him questions and record the answers, and then present them to the world.

Buddah is the King of the Run-On Sentence for a reason.

So… I'm really sorry. But admit it, a lot of you asked for his book. It's your own fault.

3

~~INTERVIEW~~ CONVERSATION

WITH A PEST

[MAX IS IN BOLD TYPE; BUDDAH IS IN REGULAR]

All right, furball. Our online friends have questions for you, since you're rarely online these days. Are you ready?

This is exciting! I've never been interviewed before and I'm not sure what I should expect but I thought a lot about the things I might talk about while I was taking a bath so that I wouldn't waste time by having to stop and think even though you keep saying "Buddah, stop and think, you have to stop and think before you do things" but it seemed like that might waste some time, so I did my thinking first so I won't need to think now.

Oh, this bodes well. First question...well, I misplaced the names of who asked what question—apologies for that—but let's do this anyway and see what happens. "What's the earliest memory that you have? Do you remember the shelter, or coming home?"

That was the place I lived before the Other Dad and I picked each other, right? In the box with bars where people kept peeking in and saying, "Ooh how pretty!" and they fed me and cleaned my box but no one let me out even though I asked like a billion times because that box was not big enough to run in or even jump around and there were other kitties in it so it felt even smaller? That was the shelter. Huh.

I don't really remember it because I was only a few weeks old and probably didn't remember anything from one day to the next, but my brain keeps telling me how I lived one place with my mom kitty and then people came and we lived another place and then one day other people picked me up and took me outside, and a bunch of us went to the place where the Other Dad pointed and said "that's the one" because everyone else looked the same and I was the only black kitty and I was pretty, but I also think my brain tells me I know that because I've heard the story eleventy million times.

The first thing I *really* remember is this nice red toy that magically appeared under the door in the Other Dad's room, like, I stuck my front leg under it so I could wave it around to make sure someone out there remembered I was trapped inside, and the magical kitty crack fairy stuck it to my paw and when I pulled it back, I had a whole new toy and let me tell you, that was some really good nip and I spent the rest of the day playing with it and bouncing off the walls, even when it was night and the Other Dad kept telling me to stop already and *please* go to sleep, but I was having way too much fun for that, until the buzz wore off and then I crawled into the red box under the bed and snoozed until he decided *he* wanted to go to bed, which meant it was time to play with all the toys and even things that weren't toys, and then run all around the room like there was a race track, which was all kinds of fun for me but I think it ticked him off, but I was a baby so there wasn't a whole lot he could do about it because I didn't understand a lot of what he said and it was mostly *blah blah blah blah are you hungry blah blah blah* but I did calm down a little bit when he turned the lights off, and made sure I pooped in the box that was near the foot of his bed, which I'm sure he was thrilled about.

That was my nip toy, and you know it. The Woman has been looking for another for me for 14 years and no one makes it anymore.

Hey, I offered it back but when they opened the door for good the Mom picked it up and threw it away because she said it might have cooties and she didn't want you to get sicker than you already were, and you were *super* sick, even though I didn't know that and figured you were just a professional grump—and I wasn't wrong about that—and if I kept trying to play with you, you'd start liking me, and then *BAM* we'd be best buddies and could race around the apartment together, but you stayed sick for so long I think you forgot what being playful was like and decided it was nonsense and then you were all like, *get off my lawn!* and went from being 3 to being 103, which wasn't any fun.

YOU RODE ME LIKE A PONY!

Well, to be fair, compared to me you were pretty much the size of a pony, and it only made sense to jump on and see if you would race down the hall, which would have been a wicked amount of fun if you'd gotten into it but you felt really bad and I didn't know it because I'd been sick with the same thing and got over it super-fast, like about a week, even though I shot 3 inch boogers out of my nose which really grossed out the Mom and the Dad, especially when I snorted them back in before they could get a tissue.

YOU *STILL* TRY TO RIDE ME LIKE A PONY!

Well, in my brain you're still the size of a pony, even though technically you're smaller than I am and you've been losing some weight even though you get to eat like 6 times a day, which I appreciate because if you get fed, I get fed, and that means I weigh more than a bowling ball and you only weigh, like, I dunno what other balls are out there but if you were a bowling ball you'd be one of those neon colored ones meant for little kids to use with bumper lanes, when all the grownups clap and cheer because they don't have to fish the balls out of the gutters and celebrating two pins being knocked down is like a big deal, and I know that because I watch TV and I saw it on that one channel that one time and I'm kind of hoping that someday we get to go to a bowling alley because those lanes look like a lot of fun to slide down, but we'd have to make sure that no one throws any balls at the same time because I'm pretty sure that would hurt.

We're not going to a bowling alley. That would mean going outside and outside means evil intruder things, like trash pandas and vishus deer and the stabby guy. Now, come on, do you remember the apartment, aside from the Younger Human's room?

Why do you call him that? Because he's the Other Dad, like, we have the Mom and we have the Dad, and he's the *Other* Dad, and you're all, like, she's the Woman and he's the Man and he's the Younger Human and that doesn't make sense because he's not exactly young anymore, even though I suppose when you first met him he was pretty young, given how old you are, but I still think he's the Other Dad and I kinda remember the apartment but not really, just that I didn't live there very long before we moved to a house that had stairs and we got to play Thundering Herd of Elephants up and down those stairs for as many hours as we wanted to, and I liked to play it a lot while you were all, come on, we gotta nap and eat sometimes and that's where you started growling at me for no good reason at all, it was like, *Buddah's blinking so I'm gonna growl at him* and I think you wanted me to be afraid of it but really all I thought was that you were a grump.

Of course I'm a grump. I live with you. The Younger Human is married now, so what do you call his wife? I think she's His Much Better Half.

Duh, she's the Other Mom, because we have the Mom and the Dad and the Other Dad, so what else would she be, unless people get to have more than two names, so if they do I suppose she could also be the Other Younger Human but I bet she wouldn't want to be called that because it's not pretty enough and she's pretty and she also has two little dogs which makes her their dog mom so SHE'S THE OTHER MOM.

Fine, cripes, don't yell. Dood, you know the Younger Human hasn't lived with us for most of your life. Is he really another dad to you?

Well, the Dad hasn't lived with his mom for like a hundred fifty thousand years and he still calls her Mom so I don't think it matters how long you don't live with someone, they're still whatever they were to you when they were here, like when you're gone you'll still be my brother, not, like, that black and white furry thing that used to sleep under the desk and sometimes went to get someone when I got stuck in the closet or pantry even though you didn't have to, and I appreciate that because I would probably still be stuck in that closet since no one ever opens that door, just that time a couple years ago when the Mom was looking for something and I darted in and she didn't see me, so she wouldn't have thought to look in there when she realized she couldn't find me.

So you're basically admitting I saved you. In some cultures, that means you have to do my bidding for the rest of your life.

Maybe, but it would really be the rest of YOUR life since you're so old and if I agreed to be your minion it would only be for a little while on account of you being SO OLD and I think I could handle doing that for the little time you have left.

You do realize that in cat terms, you're an old man now, too? Realistically, you could go before I do. I might live until I'm twenty and you might sneeze and shoot your booger brains out your nose tomorrow.

Hahaha, no, you're old and fat and those two things don't go together very well and I know that because I've seen three episodes of *Doctor Oz* and he's always trying to get people to eat better and move more so they can lose some body fat because if they don't they might die earlier than they should and you fit that because you eat like 7 times a day and you sleep all the time, so I'm pretty sure you're going first.

Dood, you eat just as often as I do, and you outweigh me by at least four pounds. You're not nearly as active as you used to be. If you want to outlive me, lose a few pounds and start running around the house again.

I try running around and jumping on things, like the bookcases that lead all the way to the best UP in the house, or even the fake fireplace, but my back legs hurt sometimes and it's gotten kinda hard for me to jump the way I used to, even from the floor to the counter where the Mom puts my food, and I get really upset about it but I don't know why I can't jump the way I did because it's not like I don't run around a lot so I get exercise, I'm just not as fast as I used to be.

Yeah, I noticed she picks you up and puts you on the counter when it's time to eat. You're old, Buddah, like it or not. You have arthritis in the back part of your body, and that makes jumping hard and painful. Losing weight might

help, but the truth is that you can't outrun your age.

Maybe not, but if it catches me I'm just going to poop on it because that's what you always say to do, poop on things and then treat them to a toothy death, and then it won't bother you and people learn lessons and you get what you want, and I want to be able to jump up and down without it hurting, because UP is my favorite thing and if I can't get to the best UP in the house I don't know what I'll do and I don't like this whole getting old thing *at all.*

Just keep trying. The People are paying attention, and when they're sure you need help, they'll make new pathways to your favorite UP spot. Maybe little ramps or stairs so you can walk up instead of jumping.

Promise?

Swearsies. You know why the bookcases in the office are arranged the way they are? The People put the ones by the window staggered like stairs so you could jump and get to the top of the tall bookcases and then my TARDIS. They didn't do it just because it looks good. And when you can't jump up those steps, they'll add more, even if it looks funky. They'll make sure you have UP until your very last day, if you want to go up.

You used to go UP sometimes and liked it but now I never see you go up, not even on the cat tree in the room with the dammit machines and you hardly ever even get on the counters to steal my treats like you used to do and I know you never *needed* UP the way I do but you used to like it, especially hiding on top of the closest in the room with the dammit machines, and I bet you would like the top of the TARDIS but you've never even tried to go see what it's like.

I don't enjoy UP the way I used to. I still like to get on the desk and snoopervise while the Woman works—she's helping me write my books, after all—and I like getting up on laps, but that's about as high as I care to go. I've never needed UP the way you do, and the People know it. But you noticed they moved the cat tree in the dammit machine room, all the way to the other side? That was so I would stop trying to get on top of the closets, because sooner or later I was going to get hurt.

So when I'm your age they might take UP away from me even though you just said they'll make sure I have UP until the very last day?

If you want UP, you'll get it. It's more important to you than it was to me, and they know that. Have you noticed all the little cubes around the house? Those are so I can still get onto the big bed and the desk. They

know I still want up there. If I wanted UP badly enough, they would make it happen. But I don't, because I don't feel safe and I really was going to hurt myself.

I thought you stopped using the tree in the dammit room because I started sleeping on it sometimes and got my cooties on it and I felt like I won something but now I feel bad because you weren't using it because it's too hard and that seems mean.

Dood, you *are* mean.

I don't mean to be mean, I just wanted to be the top kitty and own all the best spots in the house but now that I have it, it doesn't seem like I'm winning it just seems like I took something from an old man and only got it because he's not strong enough to fight back anymore.

That's nature. And I understand. I really do. But if you would stop picking on me, stop stalking and biting and jumping on me, that would be swell.

But if I stop doing that then I won't be the top kitty anymore and it keeps you on your toes and makes you alert, and that's a good thing.

You'd still be the top kitty because it doesn't matter to me. And I'd like you more.

Also, the People could turn off more lights in the house—they have them on all the time, even at night, so I can see where you are.

Why can't you see me?

My eyes are as old as I am. You're a black kitty and impossible for me to see in the dark. I was too scared to walk down the hall, so they installed an LED light so that I can see a little better, and during the day they keep the hall light on. Because of you.

Well, that means you have a fighting chance, so I don't need to stop chasing you and making sure you know I'm the One True Boss here!

See, you're mean. Don't you want me to like you?

You *love* me so I don't need you to like me.

No, really, I don't. The People love you. I tolerate you. That's the best thing we can all hope for, that we just try to live in peace. I'm not trying to hurt your feelings, but no, I don't love you.

My feelings aren't hurt but I think you're a cranky old man and you've forgotten how much you love me because if you didn't love me you would have eaten me when I was a small, helpless kitten, but you didn't, SO THERE.

I didn't eat you because you brought cooties with you and I was too sick. I nearly died.

You weren't sick that long only a few weeks and then you started eating better and started growling at me all the time but you didn't eat me so that means you love me.

By the time I felt all right—which was over a *year*, you little freak—you'd grown enough that I couldn't have eaten you. Besides, I had this dim hope that I would be able to teach you how to be a cat, but that window closed before I was well enough to do anything about it.

I know how to be a cat because I've been one my whole life and that's 14 years, and oh did you realize my birthday was a couple months ago and we didn't plan a party to celebrate it and we should because 14 is better than 13 because 13 was like being a starter teenager and now I'm the real thing!

Not to burst your bubble, but you're not getting a party.

Why not?

Because you don't have any friends. No one likes you.

You like me, and don't tell me you don't because you do.

You're high, aren't you?

Not yet but we have some really good nip toys and I was planning on batting one around the house for about 3 hours and then rubbing my face all over it so that I get the best parts of the nip, and then I can see how many colors sound has.

All of them. It has all the colors.

How do you know? Did you count them, because I tried counting them once and I couldn't get past 23 so I'm pretty sure that's all the colors there are and that's even more than rainbows have and I thought rainbows had all the colors but they don't have nice colors like hot pink or burgundy or black so whoever said that was lying or maybe they just read the wrong thing on the Internet or something.

It has the important ones. Just ask Roy G Biv. He counted and cataloged them all.

Is he on Facebook?

Probably.

I don't get to go on Facebook anymore even though I have a page and lots of friends who never get to hear from me because if the Mom isn't using the computer, you are, and by the time it's my turn she's too tired to help me so she turns it off and goes to bed and I never get to talk to anyone and they never get to talk to me, so what's up with that?

Talking to you is exhausting, that's what. I get more use of the computer because I'm working and earning money. All you're doing is talking nonstop and giving people headaches.

Well, I wanted to write a book and I thought we were going to but then you started writing about that time-traveling cat and for the last three hundred years that's all anyone writes about and I didn't get to start ANY kind of book, not even something like your book of poetry and I would be really good at poetry, but I'm never going to get the chance because you hog the computer.

Just what do you think we're doing right now, Buddah?

You're lecturing me, that's what we're doing, and let me tell you it's not very fun, and all I wanted to do was write a book so I could earn money the way you do and then I wouldn't have to wait for someone else to buy me treats and toys because I could do it myself once you show me how to find the good online stores and how to buy things.

I don't buy treats and toys. At least, not for myself. The money we make from my books goes to charity. The biggest thing we do is buy toys at Christmas for sticky people whose parents need a little help getting them stuff that year. The People buy all my treats and toys.

Well, then THAT'S why I need to start writing books, so when your brain is all mushy because it turned into an old, old mashed potato there will still be money for Christmas toys and I could do that if I would just get the chance, and I could even just do poetry or tell everyone what it's really like living with you.

They already know life with me is awesome and amazing.

Ok, so there's still poetry and maybe even a joke book!

Fine. Tell me a joke.

Go look in the mirror.

No.

But you have to because that's the joke!

Yeah, I got it. But it's not funny. Jokes are supposed to be funny. Like... okay. What time do you need to go to the dentist?

I dunno.

Tooth hurty.

I don't get it. Oh, I got one and it's a knock-knock joke. Knock knock.

Who's there?

The Doctor.

Doctor who?

YOU WISH.

Ha ha, okay, you got me. The whole world knows I like Doctor Who and plan on marrying her someday. What do you like? I'll make fun of that.

I like you.

Oh, Bast. I forgot that you think you're funny.

I am and I think you forgot you're supposed to be asking me questions because that's what an interview is, it's asking questions so you can learn about a cat or a person or even a puppy if that's who you're interviewing, though I'm not really sure why anyone would interview a puppy because what would he have to talk about until he was, like, a dog instead when he has some life experience to talk about?

What kind of life experience does a dog have that's worth talking about?

Well, they get to go outside for walks and they meet people, and if they have fun people they get to play games like fetch and Frisbee, and they know all the best places to pee and whose lawn needs a good pooping on, which you should appreciate since you have the whole pooping on things down to an art.

Still...dogs.

They're all GOOD BOYS, Max! Don't you read the Internet?

What about girl dogs?

When it's a dog GOOD BOY is gender neutral and I think you would understand that since you spend so much time playing online when you're supposed to be working.

All right, interview questions. Tell me, at what time did your train of thought derail, and were there any survivors?

I've never even been on a train but I've been in a car and that's almost the same thing except the car only ever goes two places, to the stabby place and to the M-word place and I don't like either of those.

I'm not a fan of the m-word, either. Do you even remember how many times we moved before the people bought this house for me?

It was ALL THE TIMES and I'm still upset about it because the m-word means *everything* is new and smells wrong and at first all our stuff is gone and the Mom and Dad are tired and grumpy and we don't get the attentions we deserve and then I don't want to eat because my tummy hurts and why couldn't we stay in the first place we lived? It was nice and had a long hall for playing THoE and the bedrooms were big enough for everyone, and we got our very first cat tree when we lived there.

We moved from the first place you remember because the rent got hiked enough that the people could rent a house for less money. But I moved lots before you were even born, and I was only three when they brought you home.

You were almost four but that doesn't change that we should have just stayed there where we could see things out of the windows and smell stuff coming from the people upstairs and the Other Dad lived with us for a little bit.

That stuff you smelled was illegal at the time and it didn't smell good at all. Do you even know what it was?

It was stuff growing outside and they were taking care of it and I remember that because the Woman said they were weeding, like people do when they have flowers or vegetables that they want to take care of until stuff grows big and then they kill it and eat it even though vegetables don't taste as good as cheeseburgers.

No, just...forget it. Do you remember how many times we moved?

Eleventy.

Close enough. You've moved five times if we include going from the shelter to living with us. I've moved nine or ten times.

Can't they make up their minds about where to live and why is this *your* house?

When they got me, the Man was in the Air Force and they moved him a couple times. After they got you and we moved from the apartment to the house, and we wound up moving a few more times because the houses they rented kept getting foreclosed on. So they uttered a few things off the bad word list and decided it was time to buy a house. And this is

my house because I earn a living and help pay for it, and because the Woman promised this is the last house I'll live in.

You're gonna finish paying for it before you run off to the Bridge, right?

Probably not, but maybe half of it. But don't worry. They'll pick up my slack and pay for the other half.

Then I really do need to write a book so I can help and then it will be the last house I live in, too, because I don't ever want to move again, not when I have my best UP places here and lots of places to sleep and the fireplace where all the warms live.

It better be a damned good book if you want to make that much money.

You can help me write it before you go off to the Bridge and then it'll make lots of money and we can give it to the People and tell them it's for the house so that we never have to move again and then they never have to move again and this can be their last house, too!

Yeah, I'm not sure that's what they want. They've talked about moving after we're gone, so they can live closer to the Younger Human and his Much Better Half. Anyway, at this point if you write a book the money will go for buying

toys, like my money does. At least I hope that's what you'll do. Carry on my legacy.

Are we really gonna die here in the house?

I hope so.

Do we really have to die?

Everyone does, eventually. It's not something you need to be afraid of. When we die, we get to go to the Bridge, where all our friends are waiting. And Hank the Dog will be there, and Dusty, the Cat Who Came Before Me.

Will they even know who I am?

They'll know.

But they never met me.

I think they know, anyway. And if they don't, it's still not something you need to worry about. When I get there, Hank will remember me and he's probably told Dusty about me, and I'll tell her about you. We'll be there waiting for you.

What if I go first? And don't tell me I won't because you said that could happen and you don't lie about big stuff and this feels like big stuff.

It could happen, but I don't think it will. But you still don't need to worry, because we have a bunch of friends who are there now, and they've probably met Hank and Dusty and have told them all about you. Oh, and Ataturk. That was the Woman's cat when she was little. I really want to meet her. She was so awesome that even big dogs were afraid of her.

Did the Dad have a cat when he was little?

He had a dog named Bridgette. We'll get to meet her, too.

Do you think after we're gone that the Mom and Dad will get another cat and we'll get to wait for him at the Bridge, too?

They've said they don't want more pets, at least not for a few years. We've been so awesome that it feels like we're the last ones. But I bet in a year or two they get a dog. The Woman's heart wants another dog like Hank, even if she won't admit it.

Did you really mean it when you said I was an old man, too?

You're 14, dood. In cat years, that's like being a senior citizen. But it comes with perks: the People think that old men should get anything they want, so for the most part they cater to your whims.

How old were Hank and Dusty and Ataturk?

Ataturk was 15, and she went to the Bridge after fighting cancer. Dusty was 13 when she went, but she had a heart problem. She shouldn't have lived past 6, so all those years were a gift to the People. Hank was also 13, and he had cancer, too. The People had the stabby lady help him go to the Bridge, because he was in a lot of pain.

That was nice of her.

If you or I wind up in a lot of pain, they'll help us, too.

Does it hurt?

Helping us? No, it doesn't hurt. Before they help you go, they give you a medicine that makes you sleepy and relaxed, so you leave with nice feelings and thinks.

Promise?

Swearsies. Now come on, I didn't mean to make you sad. Let's look at some questions our friends online had for you. Like this one. "How did Buddah get his name?"

Oh! The Other Dad gave me my name and he named me after this really smart and nice guy but the Mom thought I wasn't nice enough for it so she switched a couple of letters and then one of her friends suggested she add 'Pest' because I was always bothering you, and that's how I became Buddah Pest!

I hope you appreciate that. Before the Pest was added, you were Buddah Butt.

That's all right because before I learned your name you were Fat Cat.

I read your blog, you know. You said I was the Big Kitty.

Same thing.

Speaking of your blog, someone wanted to know why you never write in it anymore.

That's your fault because you write SO MUCH that the Mom said it was getting too hard to help with your krap and then pile my krap on top of it so YOU GOT TO WIN and that wasn't fair because I have a lot to say and nowhere to say it and I know I have friends online that miss me and want to hear from me, too.

To be fair, helping you write is exhausting.

That's only because she's old and has a hard time keeping up with ANYTHING.

Oh, dood, that is *so* going into this book. Okay, next question. "How do you like living with Max? Is he fun?"

I don't like this question because if I answer it I'm gonna sound mean and if I lie everyone will know it and you'll be upset either way and I have to live with you!

Just tell the truth. That's always the best thing.

Ok, fine, I like living with Max because I don't want to be alone but he's NOT fun and he's grouchy all the time, and he won't even let me jump on him or curl up on the same cat tree with him, and he GROWLS at me and THAT'S NOT FUN.

Maybe if you didn't try to ride or bite me all the time.

Well, when I was little you looked like a horse so I thought it was worth a try and it made you so mad I figured I'd keep trying because you didn't like me anyway, so why not?

Then why do you bite me?

I just want your attentions!

A gentle head bonk would do that. If you were nicer to me, I'd probably be nicer to you.

Well, I would have been BUT NO ONE TAUGHT ME HOW TO CAT.

DOOD. I was too sick for the first few months you lived with us. And we've covered this already.

Why did they take me from my mom cat so early?

To save your life. You and your littermates were in a kill shelter and had run out of time, so the SPCA swooped in and saved you. They were pretty full up, so they needed to find you a good home.

You mean the first shelter was gonna KILL me?

No one likes it, but it happens.

Okay, so that means I can't be mad that I didn't learn how to cat because you were too sick and if I stayed with my mom I might not be here at all anymore and I like being here. So.

Dood, you're allowed to be upset about the possibility even though things turned out well for you. Appreciate what you have and don't chew on the things that happened, but it's okay to have a sliver of unhappiness or uneasiness about things. Just keep it tucked away.

Like pretend it's not there?

No. If you do that, it will make you really unhappy. When you think about it, admit to yourself that it makes you sad. That doesn't mean you have to be sad all the time, though. Just...you're allowed to feel anything you feel.

I feel confused.

And that's perfectly normal for you. Okay, next. Someone wants to know what makes you purr, and what kind of pets do you like best?

Oh oh oh my favorite thing that makes me purr is when the Dad wakes up and he comes out and sits in his chair and I jump up and lay across his chest, though I'm really trying to get to his shoulder and he says I'm just too big for that now, but I do that every day and sometimes even when he's just watching TV and we cuddle and I purr because it's the best time ever.

You used to sit on shoulders when you were a kitten. And you also used to suck on the Woman's earlobe.

Oh no...did she get mad?

Nah. She knew you weren't properly weaned from your mother, and it was kinda cute. She got you to stop before your big teeth

came in. What about pets? Where's your favorite spot to get petted?

When I'm sitting on the Dad.

No. I meant *on* you. Like, do you prefer the people pet your head or your chin? Do you like long body strokes?

Oh I really like getting skritches on my head and under my collar and my chin, but only for a little bit because then I feel like I need to bite and that makes everyone unhappy.

When you bite, you get the pointy finger wagged at you.

I know and that makes me feel really bad, so I yell and try to bite again and use my claws, and then everyone is REALLY mad and I don't know what to do so I try even harder to bite and then no one wins.

The Woman is a little bit afraid of you because of that, you know.

Then she needs to stop showing me her pointy finger!

She only does that because she doesn't want to hit you. When you bite, a person's normal reaction is to lash out. Since the house

rules are No Hitting, she wags her finger. It doesn't hurt you, you know.

It hurts my feelings.

Fine, snowflake. Next question. "Do you like steak as much as Max?"

No one likes steak as much as Max because he likes food a lot, and he likes a lot of people food like real live dead fresh chicken and shrimp and tuna and steak, but I don't really like people food except for tuna water and when the Dad grills a steak for Max I like it when it's fresh and warm but I don't like it the next day after it's cold even if the Mom heats it up in the zap box.

You're not missing much. I eat it, but the Woman is lazy and doesn't take the seeds out before she warms it up for me.

At least the seeds are pretty!

Yeah, they're not too bad. Orange and pink. But I'd rather have seedless food. The seeds taste like…medicine.

She must love me more because mine never has seeds in it.

Dood, it probably does but since you never seem to chew, you'd never know. Ok,

here's another one. "Where's your favorite hiding place, and how long have you hidden there without detection?"

That one is easy because it's part of the best UP *ever* and you even like it because it looks like the TARDIS from *Doctor Who* which is your favorite thing in the whole world, and the best part of it is the top has these little sides and when I get up there and take a nap, no one can see me there since it's so high up, and I think I've been there for eleventy hours, or maybe four, but they have to get a ladder out to see if I'm up there and that's always funny because they're like, "Oh thank bast, you didn't get out."

Do you remember hiding under the blue plastic tomb when we were moving from one house into another one right next door? The house was totally empty and the door to the room we were in didn't stay closed. They found me checking out a closet downstairs and couldn't find you—and the doors downstairs were open.

I kinda remember that because I was scared and the tomb was the only place to hide so I wiggled under it and took a nap, and the next thing I know the Dad is yelling out the window I FOUND HIM after I came out to see what he was doing, and then I got lots of hugs and we went back to the other house and had crunchy treats and then got to stay there the rest of the day while they kept taking things next door.

Yeah, the Woman CRIED when they couldn't find you in the new house. It was over 100 degrees and you'd never really been outside, so she was sure she would never see you again. You were missing for over two hours.

That was a good nap.

The Internet yelled at you for scaring the People and making her cry.

The whole Internet?

The important part, all the cat bloggers. Next. Cripes. "What does Max smell like?"

Hahahahaha he smells like old cat food and desperation.

Be nice or I'll tell them what you smell like.

I probably smell like cat spit.

Change just one letter in that, dood. Fine, let's keep going. "What's your favorite surface to sit on?"

The Dad!

Do you sing or dance for food or treats?

I yell really, really, *really* loud until someone says, "Jebuz, Buddah, they can hear you all the way downtown" and then they open a bag of crunchy treats for me.

Least favorite noise?

I hate the sound of NO.

Yeah, me too. Are you a pack animal or more of a solitary creature?

I dunno, I've never had to pack for anything unless the m-word counts and then the Mom and Dad did all the packing for me but I don't think they were very good at it because I'm pretty sure a few of my toys got left behind because I never saw them again and I'm still pretty cheesed off about that even though I did get new toys.

Favorite source of heat?

The fireplace in the living room even though this year it hardly ever got turned on which makes me sad because it's the best kind of warm, all blowy and toasty and now I want to figure out how to get the Mom to turn it on even though it's not cold at all.

Remind me tonight. I'll figure it out.

No one ever sits in that room anymore so it's never on and that means there are no toasty laps to sit on while we watch TV and it's just not the same since they moved the TV to the other room with the fake fireplace that doesn't blow warms out the bottom it just blows them out the top so the room gets warm but not the spot in front of it where I like to stretch out and bake, and it all seems kind of mean.

They didn't move things around to be mean. They just like to rearrange every couple of years. They'll move it back soon. It's a people thing.

It's stupid.

Rearranging things gave you your favorite UP.

That was nice.

There's no pleasing you.

Well, sometimes they move stuff and it feels mean and stupid, like I heard them talking and they're going to get rid of the cat tree in the dammit machine room and I like to use that and you used to use it every day until I discovered I liked where it was and now it's like, *ew Buddah cooties, I don't wanna get on that* even though most of the fur covering it is yours and you barfed on it like twenty times so you marked it and should want to use it, but it doesn't matter because they're going to take it out and get rid of it.

Dood, that thing is like 15 years old and it's gross. It's time to let it go.

I don't want to but no one even asked me what I wanted and they're going to take it in the back yard and the Dad is going to CUT IT UP into little pieces like it doesn't mean anything and was never important and that's just wrong.

They'll probably get you a new one.

But I like *that* one and it's the first one I remember and—wait, new? Brand new, so it doesn't have your cooties on it?

They're not monsters, Buddah. Every time they've gotten rid of a tree, they get a new one. And even if they don't, you have three others.

But three isn't four and four is better especially if it's a tall one that I can use to get on top of the closets in the dammit machine room, so I can nap up there and hide and make the Mom and Dad run up and down the hall calling out my name and then someone gets crunchy treats and shakes the bag so I peek over the side and they say "Oh thank God" and I get treats just for taking a nap!

The fact that they have to search for you doesn't give you an idea of why the tree is going and a new one might not go in that room?

They have to search for you sometimes, too, and I know because I hear them going from room to room calling your name and they look under the desk and under the beds and in the closets and you never say anything like, "I'm right here" so they get all upset because shaking a treat bag doesn't work because you don't like them as much as I do which makes me think there's something wrong with you.

They get upset because I'm eighteen years old and someday when they look for me, they won't like what they find.

Hahahaha I bet they don't like what they find now because it's you.

Sure. Go low. And no, I don't like crunchy treats as much as you do. Why would I when they have steak bites for me?

Because steak is steak all the time but crunchy treats are chicken or beef or tuna or lobster or filled with cheese or taste like milk or even catnip.

Real live fresh dead steak is about the best thing ever, except maybe shrimp.

There's shrimp crunchy treats!

They don't really taste like shrimp. They taste like they *want* to taste like shrimp but wound up in the cardboard factory instead.

I ate some cardboard once when a box got left out where I could get to it and the flap was sticking up so I gnawed on it for like fifteen minutes before the Mom caught me and she said, "That's not good for you, you little shit," but I didn't care because she eats things that aren't good for her and no one takes *those* away, but she took the box and said I couldn't eat it but the joke was on her because I swallowed a bunch of it.

You're a rebel, Buddah.

I also ate some tape when it was sticking out on a box because I like tape and plastic and other sticky things but I didn't get to swallow any of it, I only got to chew on it because she heard me and took the box away and said not to do that because the tape could clog up my tummy and then I wouldn't be able to poop but I thought that was a good thing since she doesn't really like scooping poop.

Her litterbox duties were not the point of that exchange.

We should learn to use the Mom and the Dad's giant litterbox so that she never has to scoop again, she would just have to jiggle the handle thing that makes it go *whoosh*, and since she goes in there like 97 times a day she would be doing that already and then everyone would be happy.

I dunno, there are probably laws about flushing cat poop. Besides, we're too old to retrain for that. You'd fall in and I'd just jump in the tub and use that because it's easier.

The cat in your books knows how to use one and you seem okay with that.

Yeah, but he only does that when there's no choice. He has a litter box at home.

I wanna know who cleans his box at home, because he lives with a king and a queen and princes and a princess and that seems like something royalty wouldn't want to do.

I'm pretty sure that in the future litterboxes will be self-cleaning, but in a pinch his people will clean his box. They don't have servants, so they do it all, even scrubbing floors.

Don't you think that in the future everything will be self-cleaning or they'll have robots to do all the chores for them so they can just play all the time because that's what I would do, I would let my robots do all my work and then I could play.

People need to be mentally stimulated. Besides, if all people did was play, who would write code for the robots, or know how to fix them? I think people will always work because it helps make them feel whole.

The Mom says she wants to win the lottery even though she never remembers to buy tickets, so the Dad can retire, and that means he wouldn't go out at night to pass gas anymore so that means he wouldn't be working, so does that mean he wouldn't be whole?

No. He's worked since he was a teenager. And when he retires, he'll still find stuff to do. After working for over forty years, he should get to do the things he most enjoys.

I bet he makes more pens and stuff because he likes going out into the room we're not allowed in and he plays with wood and stuff that looks like plastic but really isn't and he makes pens and keychains and razors and roach clips and I don't know what those are, but the Mom laughed when she saw one.

Those aren't roach clips. They're things that people can use to help themselves put bracelets on.

The long ones are bracelet helpers but the little ones are part of a keychain and the Mom said that's totally a roach clip and she would know, and they must work because I haven't seen any roaches around here in a long time. Just that one time there was a roach in the litterbox and then she said all the things on the bad word list TWICE, and while she scooped the poop she snagged it and it got caught in the poop bag but she didn't feel bad for it since she uses bags that break down after a while and said it would have a wonderful time once it got all the way to the landfill, where all the garbage and some guy named Chad's hopes and wishes live.

Do you want to answer more questions that people asked?

Yes yes yes.

"How do you cope with Max's fame? Are you jealous of his talent and all the attentions he gets or are you good with it?"

I'm only jealous because you get to play with the computer more than I do and you get to talk to more friends than I do but I'm okay with how infamous you are and the attention people give you because your ego needs it more than mine does and I still get to hear about our friends and sometimes when you get paid you buy a toy that you let me play with, and I felt a little bad about that at first because your money is supposed to all go to toys for little kids at Christmas but then you said that nip toys aren't expensive and the Mom and Dad will add a little more to the kid toy money so that it balances out, and then you said that I should have fun while I can so I do, and then the Mom is all, Buddah, put your toys away, they're everywhere, it's like living with a toddler and that made you laugh, so it's all good.

Yeah, never put the toys away. Your job is to take them out of the toy basket and enjoy them. Her job is to pick them up.

That's why I throw up in 3 or 4 or 10 spots because it's also her job to clean it up and if I did it all in one place she wouldn't feel useful, and making her not feel useful would be inconsiderate of me.

Sure, keep telling yourself that. Okay. "Why do you favor the Man over the Woman? And what makes you so cranky? You were that way even when you were a bitty Buddah, I'll bet."

I'm not cranky, what makes you think I'm cranky?

I didn't ask it, Buddah. Start with the first part. Why do you like the Man more than the Woman?

I like them both the same but the Mom is your person and you made sure I knew that when I came to live with you, even though you let me sit on her shoulder and suck on her earlobe, but after a while I needed my own person and the Dad needed his own cat, so I started sitting on him and then every day when he got up from sleeping he sat in his chair, so I jumped up and tried to sit on his shoulder, too, but I got too big so I stretch across his chest and get pets, and he gives me crunchy treats every day before he goes to pass gas.

The Woman feeds us more often, though.

Because that's part of her job and he feeds us too if she's asleep and it's just fair that I get my own person too.

You were supposed to be the Younger Human's cat.

Yeah, well so were you and look how that turned out.

I think it turned out how it was supposed to. He got that Damned Dog Butters and hyperactive Lady, and that seems to be the perfect fit for him. Butters *really* needed him. And everyone loves them.

They could come over and play with us if

you weren't such a scaredy cat and didn't throw up when they did.

Like you want to play with dogs. They might eat you.

I'm pretty sure I'm bigger than they are so all I would have to do is sit on them and they'd learn to not eat me, and then we could play Thundering Herd of Elephants up and down the hall and that would be great fun as long as they didn't go into the litterbox room and eat things from it because I heard that some dogs do that.

Gross. But true. You never got to meet my dog, Hank. He was awesome but...sometimes he ate his own poop.

Hahahahahahahahaha! No way! For real?

For real. The best part, though, was that sometimes when he did, he came back inside and horked it all back up. One time, he did it right next to the bed where the Woman was sleeping. And the smell made *her* hork, too. She was on her hands and knees trying to wipe it up with paper towels, and =urp= she barfed on her own hands.

Well, now I'm sorry I missed that.

It was *glorious*. She used nearly a full roll

of paper towels and kept dry heaving even after it was cleaned up. All right, next question on the list. "What is the best thing about being a black cat? And the worst?"

Oh the best thing is that I can hide in the dark and no one can see me so that means I can wait at the end of the hall and you don't know I'm there and then I get to jump out at you and yell SURPRISE and sometimes you even pee RIGHT THERE in the hall!

Yeah, that's not funny. You don't jump out, you jump ON me. You're why there's a new light near the floor in the hall, so I can always see down there.

It's still funny because now you stop before going down the hall and look really hard to make sure I'm not there.

Only one of us is amused by that. And stop cornering me in the dammit machine room, too. It's mean.

You pooped on the floor and that was funny!

No one else was laughing, dood. Let's keep going. "We would like to know what is your favorite toy to play with? Also, your favorite spot to sleep?"

Hahahaha my favorite toy is Max!

Stop it.

But it is.

Fine, answer the other question.

I think my favorite place to sleep is also my favorite UP, in the Mom's office on top of the TARDIS that she and the Dad made for you, because no one can see me up there when I curl up, and the warm air blowing thingy blows warm air there when it's cold and when it's hot it blows cool air and I'm nice and comfortable.

Yeah, if they'd made it six or seven years earlier I probably would have liked it, too.

I'm sorry. I know it was supposed to be for you to look at but I really, really like sleeping on it and I would share it with you if you thought you could get up there.

It's fine. At least I get to see the TARDIS in the house every day. Okay, here's a good one. "If you could be anywhere you wanted, where would you have an adventure?"

Does it have to be a real place or can it be a made up place?

Anything you want.

If I could go anywhere I'd go to the Saint Francis in your books and have an adventure inside the simulator you wrote about, so that I could take a ride on Jeff the dragon and then play with Fluffy the giant cat, and we would chase sprites but we wouldn't try to eat them or even be mean to them, we'd just play tag and run through the woods and climb trees and then when we were tired we would go to the beach and lay on the sand and feel the warms from the sun licking our furs, and then Fluffy would purr really hard so the ground got all rumbly and it would be like someone purring for us, too.

Dood, that sounds kind of like the Bridge.

Maybe, but I don't think Jeff will be at the Bridge because he's pretend and will stay alive forever in the books, and I hope no real dragons are there because they might not understand that kitties aren't food and I don't want to become anyone's barbeque treat just when I get to the place where a lot of our friends are waiting.

If there are dragons, they'll be nice. I'm pretty sure that's how things work there.

Don't you ever want to go play with Jeff and Fluffy?

I get to play with them in my head and invent stories for them. That's just about as good.

So when you go to the Bridge, they go with you.

No, because the Woman can keep them alive here. She knows what I want to happen in those stories. And maybe you can pick it up and invent some Jeff and Fluffy stories of your own, Just... not one long 400-pages sentence.

Fixing that is the editor's job so I could tell the story the way I tell a story and she can stick in all the periods and commas and question marks where they go, right?

She could, but she'll yell at you. Or send you a sternly worded email that might make you cry. She's kinda mean like that.

Okay, then the Mom can do all that while she helps me write a story.

Sure. Whatever. Do you have a story in mind?

Maybe but it's not about Jeff and Fluffy.

You can write about anything you want.

I want to write a story about a boy and his cat who survive after a really bad thing happens and all the people he knows are gone, so he goes on an adventure to find other people and he runs into lots of cool animals and he finds food for them and does a lot of fun things and then before he knows it he's a teenager and he finally finds a whole group of people and they invite him to stay with him but he's gotten so used to being alone he decides to keep adventuring but comes back every once in a while because he needs to see people sometimes, but when he's out adventuring he saves the world from bad decisions people made before the bad thing happened.

That could work. You need to know what the adventures he has and what the fun things he does are. Also, what the bad thing was. Just don't make it zombies. That's been done. A lot.

I'll figure that out once I start writing it.

I look forward to reading it.

You're gonna be dead by then.

You don't have to wait that long, you know. Start thinking about the story. Dream about it. And when you're ready, the Woman will help you.

Can I name the cat Max?

As long as he's not an evil cat, sure. Will the boy be named Buddah?

No, I think that would make people think I was writing about the real person named Buddha and they would get all kinds of upset and I don't want to upset people, I just want them to be happy when they read my story, but not cry because you do that to people ALL THE TIME, you write about big things and make everyone FEEL things and then they cry.

Sometimes it's a happy cry.

But they still cry and people don't want to cry every single time they read a book, you know.

Does the boy already have a name?

Hm, no, but I think it will be something like Pete or Scott or Labron or Donovan or Kobe.

Let me guess. He plays basketball.

How did you know?

I'm a good guesser. Do you even like basketball?

Sometimes I like to watch it on TV because they throw the ball around and bounce it and sometimes it looks like I can catch it, even though

I'm not supposed to touch the front of the TV, so I just sit there and watch and pretend that when the ball comes at me I'm going to catch it and then bat it around the house like a nip toy.

You know those balls are as big as you are.

They look tiny on TV.

Think about it. The players look tiny, too.

Oh.

You can still pretend. It's not like you're actually going to get the ball.

Maybe Santa will bring me a basketball, only it will be a small one that I can play with up and down the hall in the middle of the night when I won't be getting in the Mom or the Dad's way, and if I'm lucky it will bounce a lot and I can try to make it bounce right into the toy basket, and then I can take it out and do it all over again.

Well, you'd certainly be playing basketball.

I really would! That would be fun!

I'll try to help you remember when you write your letter to Santa this year.

That doesn't sound greedy, does it?

No, it doesn't. It's only one toy. You're allowed to want stuff, Buddah. You can ask him for several things, but you'll only get a couple of them.

That's okay, because I have a lot of toys but I don't have a basketball, and that would be a lot of fun, as long as it doesn't mean that some little kid doesn't get a toy, because if it does I'll ask the Mom and the Dad to get me one instead do Santa can give the other one to a sticky person.

Look online. If you can find one, I'll buy it for you.

You have to help me online, because I never get to use the computer and I'm not sure where to look or how to buy anything.

Just go to Amazon. They have everything.

Do you have plastic money with numbers on it, because I've seen the Mom buy things online and she has to use plastic money and I think those numbers are important.

I'll borrow hers. She won't mind fronting me the money. She can take it out of my earnings.

You should go online and buy her something on account of she helps you write your books and she has to deal with the Battleaxe and I don't even know what that means but it sounds scary and she has to do it like 5 times with every book you write.

You know those times packages come and she's all, "When the hell did I order that?" Well, surprise, lady. Hahahaha.

What's the Battleaxe?

That's what she calls our editor, Tracy. She's not trying to be mean. They call each other names because they think it's funny.

What does the Battleaxe call her?

Pinky, for the most part. Sometimes she calls her Beast, but not in a mean way. It's like… she's the Pink Beast, destroyer of running shoes and miles while she trains for her breast cancer walks. It's like when the Woman calls you BooBoo and calls me Puppy. It's not mean. It's just what people do.

I like being called BooBoo. Do you like being called Puppy?

At first, I was offended. But then I realized that she *really* likes puppies, and I do tend to

follow her around the house. She means it as a nice thing. I'm her puppycat.

It's like how you call the Other Dad the Younger Human, right?

Pretty much.

If you could be called anything you wanted, what would you be called?

Hey, I'm supposed to be asking the questions.

I know, but maybe this isn't really an interview but instead we're just talking like people do.

Yeah, fine, that works. And I would be Stormageddon. Like the little kid in Doctor Who.

I thought you would want to be called Doctor.

Right now, the Doctor is female, and if I'm the Doctor she probably wouldn't want to marry me. And I'm telling you, she's going to. Besides, Stormageddon is Dark Lord of All. I like that. It speaks to the blackness of my soul.

If we were in Doctor Who, who would I be?

You'd be Mickey. At first, everyone thought Mickey was this average kind of guy, maybe a little bit like a loser, but it turned out that he was pretty tough and went on to do amazing things. He met Martha, who was another badass companion, and they got married and went on to fight the bad guys.

You think I'm tough?

I think that once you get past being the youngest here, if you try hard like he did, you could be a tough, but nice guy. You just have to stop stalking me and biting people. Really, right now you're more of a psychokitty than I am.

Can I name the boy in my story Mickey?

Sure. Names can't be copyrighted. You can use it.

So it would be Mickey and Max going on adventures and being heroes!

That would be spiffy.

Can Max be a tuxedo cat like you or should he be a different kind of kitty?

He can be anything you want. But when I started writing Wick, I decided that he should

be every kitty who was reading. If you want to know what he looks like, check the mirror.

Does he look like you in your head?

No. And I'm not going to tell you how he looks like in my head, because I don't want to change what you see when you read those stories. Be Wick when you read them.

What about people when they read your books, because they can't pretend to be them.

They should imagine their own cat. Or if they don't have one, the cat of their heart.

Okay, I won't say what I think he looks like so that I don't ruin it for all the kitties who think he looks like them, because that's kinda cool and since Wick is awesome, he should look like every kitty.

You can still describe your Max when you write your story, if you want. He could look like me. He could look like you.

Can he look like Luxor, Wick's friend?

Sure. But you know, Lux was based on another cat I knew from his blog, and his name was also Luxor. He was a sweet, beautiful, bright white kitty who went to the Bridge a long time ago.

I want book-Max to be kind of like you but look like Lux, so is that okay?

Dood, I would be honored if you wrote about a cat like me who looks like Lux. He was so nice. He also had big, fruit-bat ears that made him look both innocent and wise.

I don't even know how to get started other than thinking a lot about the boy and that he used to play basketball before everything turned bad, and that he has a cat and they go on adventures, so maybe you can help me with that, how to start?

That's how I start. With a little bit of an idea. I think about who the main characters are, and how old they are, what they look like. Sometimes I write little biographies for them, and I figure out everything I can. Like, the Emperor. I knew he was going to keep his real name a secret and that when he touched people, he could read their minds, but he didn't want them to know that.

So then he just made sure he never touched anyone so that they could keep their thinks private?

Sure, but also so they couldn't hear what was going on inside his head. It's a two-way thing. And then I figured if he wasn't touching anyone, he would be single. Maybe a little

lonely. And super smart, but not, like, *too* smart. He had to be able to make mistakes.

He talks like a history teacher, that's what you said in the books.

He tries to use proper grammar, but he also tries to be like everyone else...and he's got a Scottish accent that comes and goes, so it kinda makes him sound like a history teacher. But the point is, I try to figure out most of the little details about the people in the story before I start. And then the actual story is mostly an answer to "What if?"

Like what if there was a cat who can talk to some people and who lives a long, long time, and there's time travel and stuff, and the world is going to end so there's stuff going on that most people don't even know about because it's a secret, and along the way everyone gets to know that the one guy can understand the cat and he's not who they think he is and stuff like that?

Yeah, stuff like that. When you write a story, you're answering a question without actually asking it. And along the way, there are other questions that pop up, and you answer those, too.

What if I write the story and it's really, really bad and no one wants to read it or I'm embarrassed to let them?

The first draft always sucks. You get to rewrite it and make it better. But even if you just can't make it any better, as long as you enjoyed writing it, then it was worth the time and the effort. Then you write another story. And another. Practice until you write well, or at least write something people want to read.

Do you dream about your stories?

Not really. But I often think about them while I'm falling asleep, and I get my best ideas then, I think.

You sleep a lot.

And I get a lot of great ideas. Maybe that's what you need to do. Sleep more. Like, twenty-three hours a day.

I might miss dinner, then.

You'll hear when the can pops open. I hear it when I'm asleep.

No, you don't, most of the time if you're asleep when it's time to eat the Mom has to go wake you up and ask you if you're hungry, and that means I wind up waiting an extra five minutes because it takes you forever to get up and be awake enough to walk to the kitchen and eat, and I think you want me to sleep more so that you don't have to see me as much.

You're pretty smart sometimes.

Thank you!

You're also a bit irony-impaired.

That's because I don't have thumbs so I can't use an iron, but even if I could the Mom would never let me go near it because I might get burned, and besides, I don't think we even HAVE an iron, but if we do it's probably all rusty since no one ever uses it.

I totally understand. But you know, she wouldn't mind if you picked up your toys now and then.

Didn't you say that was her job?

Did I? Well, no, it's not *really* her job. She just winds up doing it because you scatter them all over the house.

That's *my* job and if she doesn't like it maybe she should just leave things where they are so that I can play with them some more and not have to dig them out of the toy basket.

I thought you liked digging in the toy basket.

I do because it's a lot of fun to stick my head in and sniff all the nip toys and then pick one up and toss it out because it's a good toy but not the toy I'm looking for and then I get to do it over and over until I get to the one I want, and if I get the one I want too fast I set it aside so I can find it later and then everything is more fun.

Maybe you'd have just as much fun gathering up all the toys and putting them back.

That sounds like work.

Yet you want to be a writer. That's work, dood. Like, a real job.

Writing stories is just making stuff up and making stuff up is fun and not work, so maybe you're doing it wrong.

Writing the story is only part of it. When you finish, you still have to fix all the problems with it. Sometimes, you wind up rewriting the whole thing.

But you're still making stuff up and that's fun.

Dealing with edits and having to cut out your most favorite parts of a story is not fun.

That's the Mom's job.

I'm starting to understand why she loves Fireball so much.

I know, right? She has a TON of it, like, a little bottle on her desk and one in the freezer, and two GIANT bottles on the thingy where all the stupid drinks live, but I think the biggest bottle was a present, so I'm not sure that counts, but she has WICKED amounts of Fireball.

And I'm sure she wants the world to know that.

Okay, well then maybe she wants it to know she also has a GIANT bottle of Irish whiskey that she brought home when the Other Dad got married, and there's THREE kinds of vodka, and another bottle of stuff that's like Fireball but isn't, and there's a bottle with a captain on it, and another I heard her say is a math problem but I don't know how.

It's to make a drink called a Seven and Seven. And it's not all for her. Mostly it sits there to look good. I don't remember the last time I saw either of the people take a drink.

There was a lot of drinking at Christmas or maybe it was after or before when the Other Dad was here with the Other Mom, and the Grandma came here, and they had pizza, and the Mom had Fireball and I'm pretty sure the Other Dad and the

Other Mom had drinks, but not the Grandma and I don't think the Dad had one, on account of he had to drive the Grandma home.

There were a few drinks, not a lot.

Which one is the bottle with the LEGAL WEED in it?

There isn't one. It's not a drink. It's something a person either smokes or has in a special treat that they eat, and there isn't any in the house.

Are you sure about that because when the talking head on TV said that it was allowed for people to have now the Mom said LEGAL WEED a *lot*.

Because she thought it was funny.

Really? Why?

She thinks she's funny. No one wants to hurt her feelings and tell her she's not.

Well, if she's gonna help you edit this she's gonna find out.

No worries. I'll get the Man to read it first and he can hide the parts that will hurt her feelings.

You like to write about big stuff sometimes so maybe you can write and make her feel okay about it.

What kind of big stuff?

Well, you wrote that thing about the Rainbow Bridge in your *Mousebreath* column when Hershey the cat was scared about his cancer, and that was kind of big and made people cry but in a good way, and then in one of your books you wrote about a kid named Jimmy who started going by Jay who's trans even though I don't know why, and you write about a man with special needs and he's one of my favorites because I feel like I relate to him.

I wrote about Jay because the Woman has a few transgender friends, and their story is important. I was hoping I could make it seem like, even though it's important and it's this huge journey some people have to take, that no one needs to be upset by it. They helped a lot, too, telling me what they wished and needed. I hope I got it right.

The Mom said it was a touchy subject and might make some people stop reading your books.

I know. And it might. There are a lot of people who don't want me to be liberal on anything, even though I'm pretty much apolitical and middle of the road about most things in life.

Did writing about a special needs man upset anyone?

So far, I don't think so. Hyrum is wonderful and sweet, and I wanted to make it clear that he's perfect the way he is. People understood that. A few have asked me what's wrong with him...but there's nothing wrong. He's not broken and doesn't need to be fixed. Hyrum is the toughest person in the Wick universe, I think, but he's so gentle and sweet that it's easy to forget that he walked across the country by himself and never gave up.

I didn't like his mom.

She's not supposed to be likeable, but I think she's relatable. Remember, she had a lifetime of oppression living with a tyrant, and she never had a day to herself because Hyrum needed supervision and protection. All her kids did. She's tired, and deep down she's conflicted between wanting the freedom to be herself and her belief in her religion, which tells her she's not allowed to do anything other than what she's told.

But then Hyrum lives with Aubrey and Jax and they don't seem tired.

Aubrey has an entire support system, and she doesn't have to live with the idea that she's

her husband's property. Hyrum's mother had no one, really. And that happens a lot in real life...people feel stuck with the lives they have, and they don't see a path they can get on that will make them feel free. Not everyone has the resources to lift themselves up. Valerie Munson didn't, and she didn't have the education or experience to understand there are other lives one can lead.

If you were a person you'd go to school all the freaking time, wouldn't you?

I think I would have gotten as much of an education as I could. That doesn't mean going to school. There are hundreds, maybe thousands, of ways to get an education.

You mean reading, right? You're always wanting to read stuff.

That's one way. Experiences are an education, too. Face it, you can read a lot about cars, but it's getting your hands dirty and taking them apart that teaches you the most. If you can find someone who knows the things you're interested in, you can learn a lot. About anything.

What do I do to learn about writing?

Read. Yeah, this is one where reading is the answer. Read a lot. Every day. Read books

the way people breathe air. A good writer reads. And don't listen to the Internet. A lot of people there will tell you that you can be a good writer without being a reader, but they're wrong.

Can you be any kind of writer if you don't read?

Sure. Anyone can write for themselves, but to be a good writer, you need to be a reader, too.

What if you're wrong?

That's not a position I'll ever waver from. There's a saying: is this the hill you want to die on? I'll totally die on that hill. Reading is that important.

I better start reading then, because right now all I really do is watch TV and I like it a lot, especially the stuff where people are running or there are tigers, and the best thing would be a show where people are running from tigers, but that might not be nice because I kinda want the tigers to win.

The tigers would totally win.

But if the tigers win then all the people watching will get upset and there's gonna be a lot of blood and guts, and then they'll yell at the TV people, and they'll never show tigers on TV again.

Them's the risk.

Oh, maybe you can write a story where there's a giant tiger, and he chases people and eats a few, and that's how he became a giant, because people meat is super good for a tiger and then people start thinking, hm, maybe we should eat each other and see if it works, and in the end there are giant people.

Dood. Just...no. Besides, you know what happens when a tiger eats a person? They shoot him.

Shoot him dead?

Yep.

Well, that's not nice. So maybe in the story you can have a world where there aren't any guns or knives so they can't kill the tiger, and then they get to find out about people meat.

All right. Then how do people kill other people so that they can eat the meat?

Toss a toaster into the bathtub and then the person would be dead AND kinda cooked.

You are seriously messed up, Buddah.

But I bet people would like to read that story because people like scary things and that seems really scary to me.

Horror is a genre. It might be a better movie than a book, though.

Oh! And then I could root for the tiger!

Sure. Whatever your little black heart desires.

Right now it desires something to eat but I don't think it's snack time.

It is not. Go back to the writing thing. If you could write a story in the Wick universe, what would you write?

Oh! If I wrote a story it would be in outer space because it's science fiction and that means space and stuff about space, and I think I would send someone to that space station to do things and then other things would happen and they'd be all OH NO THIS IS WRONG and then other things would happen and they'd be all WE SHOULD STAY ON EARTH, but Wick figures it all out and they all live happily ever after.

You'd have to figure out what things happen.

I might need help with that part.

I have a few ideas. Hell, I even have notes about Drew in space.

How do you come up with ideas?

Most of the time they just come to me. Sometimes I see just a little bit of something, and it fires off in my brain and the story starts to form. That's how the Woman got the idea for the last book in her *Charybdis* series. She was taking a walk, on a bike path that was shaded by a bunch of trees, and at the end of the path the sun was super bright and she got this image in her head of a bench by a pond, the water glittering like diamonds. And right after that she thought about two of her characters on that bench...and one of them is a dead guy that she killed off in the first book. It turned out to be the best book in the series.

She says she wants to rewrite the first book.

I know. And maybe someday she will, once she figures out how to do it and not lose the reviews she already has for it on Amazon.

Do you get reviews?

A few. I think people don't understand how important good reviews are to a writer's

career, so they don't take the time to leave one. That doesn't mean they don't like my books, though.

I'll review them if you want.

I appreciate that, but your reviews would get deleted. The big stores don't allow friends and family to leave reviews. And I agree with that. It only becomes an issue when someone you're only remotely connected to has a review deleted.

That's not very nice.

That's the way it is.

There should be a place anyone can review books.

There might be, but I'm unaware of it.

Oh! That can be my new business! Buddah's House of Reviews!

Without standards, though, the trolls will come out in droves just to leave bad reviews for writers they don't like. Even if they never read the book. And some writers will leave bad reviews for other writers just because they're competition.

Well, that's not very nice, either.

For someone who's frequently not-nice, I'm not sure why it bothers you.

Just because I annoy you and sometimes try to ride you and bite you and take your lunch when you take a break to go get a drink that doesn't mean I'm not fair.

I think eating someone else's lunch is the definition of unfair.

No, that's opportunity presenting itself and that's not being mean, it's just being hungry.

Look at you, using big words.

I think I have to if I want to be a writer.

Not necessarily. There's another saying: never use a dollar word when a nickel one will do.

WORDS COST MONEY?

No, it means... fine, sure, they cost money and I'm the word-treasurer. You can pay me for all the dollar words you want to use.

But I don't HAVE any.

Here's a thought. Pick up your toys every day and maybe you'll get an allowance.

That still sounds like work.

Being a writer is work. It's a job. If you don't want to work, you won't be able to write a book.

It doesn't look like work when you do it, it just looks like a lot of talking and a lot of thinking and talking more so the Mom knows what you want her to type but you never get up and like DO anything.

Trust me. It's still work. And you sit there and listen a lot...what's your favorite part of listening?

I like hearing the story before anyone else and getting to see how you think things up and change things and how you sound like Max one minute and Wick the next, but I'm not as happy about listening to the bouncy parts because that seems like really grown up things and, oh boy, I DIDN'T KNOW PEOPLE COULD BEND LIKE THAT, but I really like it when you write about Hyrum because he's my favorite.

I always thought you would like Jeff most of all. In *Forked* he was a sleek black baby dragon and in my head he kind of looked like a dragony version of you.

I didn't know that! I like Jeff and I like Fluffy but Hyrum is nice and sweet and he just wants to be good and for people to love him, and he tries really hard, but sometimes he gets frustrated and I know how that feels. Is he going to grow up?

I think Hyrum will make some very big leaps, but he'll also remain very much the same. I don't ever want him to lose that sweetness or even the innocence that he managed to hang on to despite the horror of his childhood. Hyrum is that part of us that should never change, the part we need to hold onto.

What part of us is the Emperor?

I think he's the adult we need to be. The one who can make the hard decisions and who is willing to show up and do the work. He'll do anything for the people he loves and has a lot of compassion for everyone else—but that won't stop him from doing what needs to be done. He's the part that looks to the greater good and does what's best for everyone. He tries, anyway.

If you could be anyone in your books, who would you be?

Hard choice. On the surface I want to be Drew. He's super smart and creative but not elitist about it. Part of me wants to be Finn

because that dood is going to live a freakishly long time...but he makes so many mistakes and judgment errors that I also don't want to be him. I think that my ego wants to be Aubrey. She's kind of the glue that holds them all together, and she's risen above the things her father did to her, and she's just...kind.

Her superpower is making people feel better.

I prefer to think of those things as gifts. What gift would you want to have?

I want to be able to open cans anytime I want something to eat.

Good choice. I think even Wick would want that.

You know what's funny?

What?

Neither of us said we wanted to be Wick even though he's the star of everything and he's a cat, and he's super old and pretty smart and really, really important.

Huh.

I wonder why.

Probably because there's a little bit of Wick in us already.

We're really old Max. What happens to Wick when you're gone?

The Woman knows his story. All of it. She knows what I want for him, and she can help me tell those stories even after I'm gone.

Does that scare you? Being gone?

No. I know where I'm going, and it'll be fine.

Are you ever gonna write anything else besides Wick?

I'm working on poetry, too.

Can I write a poem?

Sure. I don't own the form.

Eenie Meenie Miney Mo
Catch a psycho by the toe
If he yowls he's just a kitty
Tick him off and say he's pretty

Not half bad. But I wouldn't be ticked off. I AM pretty. I'm fabulous.

I could write other poems and I could do a really good one if you'd tell me what rhymes with Nantucket.

...
...
...

Bucket. The answer is bucket.

Is it blue like the bucket that walrus online has been looking for as long as I've been alive, because it was a very nice blue and I understand why he wants it back, so whoever took it needs to just give it up already because that walrus has to be 100 kinds of sad about it and if he catches you he's gonna sit on you, and I've seen how big a walrus is on TV and that's gonna hurt.

So there's your poem. Write about the bucket.

There once was a walrus from Nantucket
And someone walked off with his bucket
He was all kinds of sad
And six kinds of mad
And when he finds it he'll say oh well—

No. Just no. No one wants to hear you say that word.

Why not? You say it and you even put it in your books.

Okay, for starters, you kind of stole that from me. It was kind of the gist in the last entry in my poetry book.

Oh. I didn't read that one.

The poem or the book?

Um...

Jerk.

Weren't you supposed to be interviewing me and not talking about YOUR stuff?

I'm pretty sure you started talking about my work first.

Yeah, well, you went on so long I forgot what we were really doing here, and that was asking me questions because this is an interview and that's what you DO in an interview, you ask questions and LISTEN for the answers and then write the answers down so that everyone else can read them.

Somewhere along the line we just started talking.

Maybe we should do that more often and then maybe you'd like me more and maybe you'd be happier and not as grumpy and we'd have fun and stuff.

Are you going to stop stalking me, jumping on me, and biting me?

No.

Well, there we go.

I'm just trying to have fun.

Only one of us is having fun in that equation.

Maybe I'll stop when I get a little older and can't bother the way you can't bother with a lot of things.

Truly, I hope I'm here for that.

Me, too, and not just because I'm the Top Kitty now, but it would be nice if we were friends someday and did things like curl up together on the bed and purr for each other.

I'd like that.

That means you have to stick around.

I'll try my best. And it also means you have to stick around, too.

How long?

As long as it takes, you little pest.

Okay. And I know you have a lot of days when you don't feel all that great so I'll try to figure out what those days are and I won't bother you and I'll stay out of your bedroom because it's your room and not mine even though I don't know how you got your own bedroom anyway.

It just worked out that way. You have the top of the TARDIS. I needed my own space.

I get that. Did anyone else have questions for me?

I went through them all.

Can I ask something?

Sure.

How come you hardly ever blog anymore? I mean, I never get to because I can't get on the computer but you don't blog like you used to and neither does anyone else and I miss reading all the cat blogs.

Honestly, I think Facebook happened. All the people who helped their cats write blogs moved over there and they started talking to each other, and some of the cats started their own pages. It even happened with people blogs. The Woman used to read dozens every day but

most of those haven't had a post in years. It's a little sad, because Facebook doesn't feel as personal as the blogging community used to.

We made real friends when blogs were big.

I know. More importantly, the Woman made some very good friends. People I think she'll be friends with forever.

Like the ladies she does boobie walks with? They were cat bloggers.

Some of them were, but she's met some other boobie walkers along the way, and they've become friends, too. But the cat bloggers are special, and I think she'll want to know them for the rest of her life.

I like that.

I do, too.

You did that, you know. If not for you she wouldn't have some of the best friends she could ever hope to have and she'll still have that even after we've gone to the Bridge.

Dood, I'm the King of making people cry. Don't try that on me.

But it's true and you know it.

I know. And remember that, Buddah. If you leave this world a better place than it was when you got here, if you find a way to make someone's life happier, and you leave them with sparks of joy, you served your purpose. It doesn't have to be in giant ways. Sometimes it's soft and gentle, and seems small on the surface...but it's important to leave something better when you go.

Will I?

You're mean, you bite, you chase...but you've also made people laugh and have given me a million opportunities to tell stories about you. People love you, and not just our people. I think you already have. You don't need to worry about doing more. Just...don't do less, okay?

I sleep a lot. I'm not sure it's possible for me to do less.

You made your mark when you weren't looking. It's all right.

I was looking, Max. And I know what you're thinking. If you go first, I'll take care of them.

I know you will. Let's hope it's not for a while.

Lunch?

Come on. I'll get the Woman to open a can of stinky goodness, and maybe there's even something real live fresh dead and delicious waiting for us. I smell something. Maybe she's cooking.

That was me. I farted.

Way to ruin a moment, Buddah Pest.

Hahahaha you love me anyway.

We've been over this. I really...you know what? I give up. Sure. Whatever. Just tell me what you've learned, the important things, and then we can go eat.

Oh. I learned lots. Poop on pillows when someone makes you mad. Or treat something they love to a toothy death. Demand food every two hours, but don't eat everything because of reasons, and never eat the Mom's meat loaf because that never ends well. Help clear off all the counters even when they ask you to stop. Kick all the litter out of the box so they don't have to dig hard to scoop it clean. Sing loudly at two in the morning when the acoustics are the best and you have a captive audience. Don't bite thumbs because thumbs are how cans get opened. Run fast. Be kind. And when someone is sad, no matter how badly you want to go take a nap, climb onto them and purr as hard as they are upset, because a good purr is soothing and can help them heal.

Good job, dood. Maybe you never learned how to cat, but you did learn, and I don't think I can ask for anything more.

Crunchy treats. You can ask for crunchy treats.

Always.

AFTER THE WORDS

By Buddah Pest

Max and I had this conversation a year ago. Now he's 19 years old and I'm 15 and I'm doing what he wanted me to do: I'm not mean to him nearly as much and I only stalk him once in a while and I don't jump on him but I did nip at his neck a few times, but I wasn't trying to hurt him, he was just there and I don't know why I did it, but here we are.

He's had a *really* rough summer, full of ouchies and sad, but he's hanging in there. At first the Mom and the Dad thought he was about to run off to the Bridge, because he had a few days where he just wouldn't eat and he barely moved, and on the worst night of our lives together, the Mom found him passed out with his face in the food dish she had left in the closet for him earlier that night. She even says she approached him sadly because she thought he was gone, but when she got really close he lifted his head and meowed a tiny, tiny meow, and she understood that he was hungry and needed help, so she held the plate for him and he finally got some food into his tummy.

He took us all on a roller coaster ride for the next 6 weeks; they did everything they could think of to help him, and the stabby lady did everything she could think of, and a lot of what they thought was that since he'd lost a lot of weight, his thyroid pills were making him sick because the dose was too high. So they cut back on that and it helped some, but the Woman was all, "There's more, he's in pain, I can tell he's in pain," but because he has bad kidneys, there's not really anything they can give him for it.

She thought he was in pain because a couple days before they thought he was dying, he tried to jump onto the footrest of her recliner and he kinda missed—he can't really jump anymore—and he landed hard. It didn't seem like it bothered him at the time but she's broken a lot of bones, which makes me thinks she's a few kinds of clumsy, and she said that sometimes the first day or two it's just ouchy and then the pain comes *roaring* at you. And right about the time she found him with his face in his plate full of fish & shrimp stinky goodness, he was right about where her broken bones hurt the most.

He couldn't walk in a straight line, and he was favoring his back left leg so much it looked like he was trying to not let it touch the floor. And when he laid down it was always on his right side. The Mom and the Dad catered to him, bringing him food when he wanted to hide in the closet and making sure there were water bowls in every room he liked to be in, and they opened a bunch of cans just to be sure they opened one he would take even one or two bites from. I did my part by staying away from him because if I went close he might start to worry that I was going to do something mean and I didn't want to make him feel worse.

Day by day, he seemed to get a little better. There were days they were still afraid he would leave us, but after about 4 weeks the Mom said she wasn't tied up in knots anymore, and didn't dread getting out of bed every morning because she was afraid of what she would find. It was like this thing settled over him and he wasn't hurting so much and he wanted to eat more and he moved around enough that the Dad built boxes for him to use as steps so he wouldn't have to jump much anymore. And then about a week ago, it was like we had Max back. His eyes were brighter and he wanted food all the time, and he wanted to sit in her lap and let her adore him. I left him alone, because I knew he didn't feel good, and I'm still mostly leaving him alone because he's an old, old man, and I'm going to be an old, old man soon and there won't be another kitty here to upset me, so I'm trying to not upset him even though he gets annoyed when I breathe.

We all understand the reality of Max's age. He's 19. He's lost half his body weight in the last 3 years or so. But I'm happy to report that as of today, September 10, 2020, he's doing really well and is eating, drinking, peeing, and pooping like a champ.

Now, if you ask him, this isn't exactly the book he had in mind, but between the 11 or 12 Wick books he's written in the last few years and the Mom's work, I'm just happy that he helped me work on something and we had a good time sitting here going over the edits with the Mom, and when he said maybe we needed to have another conversation I reminded him that' he's 19 and people have been waiting a long time.

This feels like MY first book, even though his name is on the cover and I understand why his name is on the cover, because he's THE MAX and I'm just getting started, so maybe the next one will have my name on it, too.

But mostly I wanted you to know how he's doing. I was really scared I was going to lose my big brother, even though he's smaller than me now, and even though I annoy him all the time, my life would not be anything nearly as good without Max in it, and I wanted you to know that, too.

Buddah Pest
September 10, 2020

Made in the USA
Coppell, TX
19 October 2020

39969625R00057